ROSE WIT

DANIEL HARDISTY
Rose with Harm

SALT

CROMER

PUBLISHED BY SALT PUBLISHING 2020

2 4 6 8 10 9 7 5 3 1

Copyright © Daniel Hardisty 2020

Daniel Hardisty has asserted his right under the Copyright, Designs
and Patents Act 1988 to be identified as the author of this work.

First published in Great Britain in 2020 by
Salt Publishing Ltd
12 Norwich Road, Cromer, Norfolk NR27 0AX United Kingdom

www.saltpublishing.com

Salt Publishing Limited Reg. No. 5293401

A CIP catalogue record for this book is available from the British Library

ISBN 978 1 78463 217 5 (Paperback edition)

Typeset in Sabon by Salt Publishing

Printed and bound in Great Britain by Clays Ltd, Elcograf S.p.A

To Meriwether

Contents

☿

ROSE WITH HARM

Cedar, Sandalwood, Cut Stems

Those bulbs of rain, clear and time-slowed,
that fell as you shook out your umbrella.
The storefront lights still on in the high street.

The pitching, rain-fractaled headlamps
swooping the glass as we gave the address
and the sudden scent of you, half yourself,

half perfume: like cedar, sandalwood,
cut stems, and the smell that lingers in rain
that ran so quick-fingered through me.

Rose with Harm

Isolate flower,
fast-folded clef,

promise
tight as copper coil.

Unpeeled
you waft desertion,

oils, torn grass, grape
stem in the bowl,

chlorophyll,
ketone on the breath.

You would rather
starve now

than reopen
to the sunlight.

At dusk's repose
pearling,

more lumens
than the room entire.

Not moon, not sun.
Heart generate,

white elder,
your pale

low voltage
may yet

force a shadow,
kiss

the world object.

Bride

If I were to leave unannounced,
the band still playing in the wooded glade,
the drinks on tables and the bar wide open,

you're the one I'd take my cue from.
The way you slipped out the side door,
not even collecting your coat,

walking away from the marquee in winter
into the cold, scented air;
the dresses with their backs to you,

and the brightsided tent
becoming first a far-off cinema screen
then a distant house with a single lit pane.

Always

After Neruda

Facing you
I am not jealous.

If you arrived
with a man on your back,
or a hundred men
hanging in the rigging of your hair,
or a thousand men
sleeping on the soft mound of your belly,
if you were a river
filled with drowned men
met by the furious sea
foaming at its mouth,
by eternal weather –

if you arrived with them all
where I wait for you,
I would not be jealous.
We will always be alone.
We will always be, you and I,
alone on this earth
to begin life.

Ψ

Neptune

Under the thin-laid stillness of the bath
I would practise my absence;

watch the berg of my toe
shape its own reflection in the water;

take my breathing
to the point where it might not restart

like the anvil head of the pump jack
that nods its last slow nod.

The warmth spread through my arms
like wine in another country:

where trees at the curl of the hilltop
hear the first sway of music;

the sun softens behind a milk of clouds,
the glass perspires gently.

There, in that nowhere of the self,
I'd let my arms rest beneath the water

with a puppet's acquiescence;
floating above the ocean bed

with its wrecks of needle and glass.

Mermaid

On the third day she was still alive,
caked in healing salts,
her arms jewelled as peacock feathers.
Her shallow breathing like the gentle lapping
of water in the washbowl.
My cheap cotton towels wrung and re-soaked
and laid again along her dry tail,
while the wire grill of scales
slowly found their lustre.

She slept.
I watched her like daft Narcissus in the pool.
Wiping the salt foam of her lips:
a silver fish flashed in the
black bowl of her eye.
I would live.

Birthright

For those snatched from the safety of their homes,
stolen by their stepfathers at the quarter moon
or dumped at the tower to spin silver thread;
those denied their rightful prince or palace, or found
by the blind women abandoned in the briar
and raised with a secret birthmark or royal blood;
those who watched their families and found strangers;
studied portraits to find records start at four or five;
for those secreted away before their uncles could
discover the prophecy true, the child survived;
you who suspected all at the Sunday meals,
who burned brighter, grew more gifted than the flock,
temper your shock as I confirm your misgivings;
soon you'll be too old to look at children's books,
where all the clues are hidden, and your novels
will be written by middle-aged men and women
who've forgotten when they wrestled the golden ass
from the troll at the crossroads (his name chanted
backwards three times so each could pass);
don't yourself forget so fast, detective to the last,
you are not the woman at the post office rope
or the man at his desk fixing company quotes,
even as you type you see the band of white
which denotes the ring of the royal houses lost
or might once have been, or seemed to be, or never was.

Dream

I dreamed of the yellow house in Rockport,
sober town by the sea where we smuggled
vinho verde, locked in the trunk of the car,
drinking our way through a case in days.

I had been here many times before, not days,
and a woman - standing by the bedroom door -
had waited patiently there to remind me
of something. On her face a freckle's stain,

that was a heart stain somehow, as we looked
at each other with a quiet ease. My life,
my family, seemed forgotten, pushed to one side
by the detail of one speck of lightest brown

on a face I didn't know, in that sober town.
She didn't say what message there was for me
in her look. But left me to wake and write
of love, and exclude it from my private book.

Boston, MA

Moon

A dream the night before I left for America.
A full moon,
the earth at our backs
as if it were a satchel we carried.

We waited,
like the children of believers,
to see
its bright disc:
a scalpel turned through a circle
by the measure
of a wrist.

We were mistaken
or
deceived in the dream.
The body that rose
was our own planet –

a sphere
of blue and green and white –
hanging
in the dark

like a fruit without
its tree
or branch.

Pluto

I tug the curtain to confirm
the weather I hear on the radio
the dark tear of a blackbird
against the untouched snow

Poem

i.m. C.T.

The winter light is yellow
not white,

a dusting of snow is no dusting
but a terse breath.

The street lamp stands
beyond

the window sash
unable to shiver.

There is something
to say about this:

the light above the river –
the forgery of clouds,

the huge grey and empty space –
the day your Mom was standing

at the window, still,
practicing her own absence in some way,

how she said she *used to*
care for such things, the river, the light,

but not now.
The world, as it grows nearer,

resists our reading,
the gull puncturing the white

like the nail and smudge
of a tiny hand.

Beacon, NY

Exit Wound

home sick
soil sick
sick in love again

nosferatu
leaves two
beads of blood

nippling
the naked white
of her neck

she will not live
or die
or live

at night
the wolves
howl

their short
long short
howl

my step
father told
me the wolfman

had been
driven mad
by the moon

by which
he meant
mad by women

two silver
bullets might
suffice

through the
heart
to finish him

fentanyl
and ice chips
they nipped

at my liver
with a scrapping
needle

and told
me not
to carry a book

or a daughter
for twenty
four hours

I looked
beneath
round dressings

found two distant
equal
punctures

made by silver
or tooth
incision

I imagined
an exit wound
at my back

its plume
of red
tubercular cough

and my body
blown
through

like an egg
pricked
both ends

at Beth Israel
I wait
for a car

alone
at six thirty
and laugh

that this is
how
my story ends

half in love
even now
with moon

and picture
and
brambled

men
mad in forests
the castles

the split
scientist
the risen dead

the towers
and skies
are empty

my driver
makes
small talk

as I cry
at simplicity
of speech

bluster
of morning
radio

adrift
each voice
reporting

Boston, MA

Midpoint

The four frosted panels of glass
are more the fall of light
onto a wall than a window.

In the yard's cold basin
a cord of water runs endlessly
through the hands of a fixed hose.

Beneath me, underground streams
call me by my real name
and laugh at my bed and clothes,

my man-made jeans. Here,
at night's midpoint, it is best
to avoid mirrors for fear of waking

yourself twice into the world,
a sleepwalker treading air
trapped this side of the glass.

ち

Ring

Because the ice cube
melts in my palm
and does not assemble

its small glacier
from a trickle. Because
the electron is slowing

like the clock's mechanics
and the flame and neon
will grow dark,

why not tarry
the infinite in its arc
and resolve our love

– unfuelled
by any outside thing –
that gives this ring?

Strangers

She walked out the mist
as off the big screen:
hailing us, the passing
vehicle in the scene.

Behind her, moorland,
mountains and nothing;
tears and rain burning
her relieved face.

We'd passed the afternoon
in aimless shopping.
She: wandering, lost
for hours, to this place.

Our rescue of her proved
us somehow charmed.
*She tried to press a wet
twenty in my palm.*

II.

Now time tilts the camera
the other way,
seen through the eyes
of the lost girl the day

she strayed down the wrong
side of the mountain
and was found by us,
tearful, wandering

into our brief time,
our love's unsure, uncertain
weeks, beneath the sky's
slow gathering.

What did she see
in those two strangers there,
past her cold
astonishment we now bear?

Loch Oisein

Distances

Now try to plan your journey home.
No matter where you set out from, what little
you put aside for the crossing.

Watch the city dilute into the suburbs,
the terraced houses rise to meet you
where your old clothes

hang in greys above the front yards
and the football slaps against middens,
where a stave of wickets is poised

beneath the painted goal posts,
and voices call to you in your own voice,
their names long forgotten.

Do you even recognize the place?
Here, in this rented room,
your suits creaking in the wardrobe,

the man pacing upstairs,
the night sounds as the boiler rattles to life
and the moon studies the curtain,

listen for the voices
that drift across the public grounds:
we carried on our games, there's room for you,

now tell us why no one has called us home.

The Bridge

What of the feeling built into landscape –
the me that sat below the iron bridge
in Newcastle each week, while the cold Tyne

was patrolled by ghosts, the Roman currachs,
the keels fat with coal, the late revellers
still leaving the *Tuxedo Princess*,

their last cries echoed by the quayside gulls.
There are some places we can never leave
having lived our lives too heavily there.

A wooden bench with a single duff slat,
the bin where I would toss my cigarette,
doused like the feeling that called me each time

down Queens Lane to the banks of the Tyne
in the days and months *after*, to forget.
I was mourning, not for ourselves, or by

the end even for you: but the kept sense,
I hardly even remember forming,
that love would always solve and qualify

whatever had come before. I stared out
each Sunday; sometimes the water minnowed
with light, sometimes dark herds of current

seemed in movement below the slow surface.
I kept my vigil, and see I keep it still:
each time my train pulls across the last bridge

on its long arc into the station. I look
for my dark-suited double, a daubed man –
a shadow even beside the river –

and see him at his slow work and shiver.

Aberdeen Street

The books are waiting in the hall,
they will not remember us.
Perhaps they'll find new homes

and hands that ease them open?
You were angry when I threw things away,
some value might still lurk in them.

Now the sofa, with its stains and hollows,
our daughter's clamberings,
waits for men to carry it outside;

the tent that sheltered her toys,
the rugs stretched out feline
that were, a while, the grass beneath her feet.

I'm already ghost
and yet already in some kitchen
where the stove has warmed the room

and music plays and where, for a moment,
I'll think of myself now,
on this couch in the fire glare of the TV screen,

the blinds still up,
and the street lamps come on at eight,
how I was right

that I would always carry you
and cannot join the circle
without your loneliness with me.

Boston, MA

The Train Set

The train set is built and rebuilt without care
for itself, its carriages are empty.

Tongue and groove hold together a branch line
or lay a straight track to the station.

Here no one is waiting except a lone conifer,
green as the first green of a paint set,

and an imagined passenger who rides
not knowing he is ticketless and walletless.

He will only ever arrive at this station,
unsure of where he joined the circle:

not unpleasant, not without its views
of the big-handed girl who is planning disaster

where the tracks climb and the steam rises.
Once, an old man on the train from Holy Island

asked me to search his pocket book
in the hope I might find his lost address.

He has long forgotten me. Though I flip
the lettered pages to see if I myself am home.

South Orange Grove

This is the house you came home to:
apartment block south of the Mile.
Render peeling from the stucco walls –
stripped away by the desert sands
that slept beneath the baking street.

Our driveway where you scooted, free
in your walker of green and blue
plastic, and made your socks a sole
of ash. At night the helicopters
swept up Fairfax or paused over

San Vicente and Olympic;
made the sleeping windows rattle
like a stack of china saucers,
while the floorboards cooled beneath
their polish. We had unhappiness

and brought you home to live in it,
then watched you grow above us
like a green canopy, and stretch
like desert blossom creeping through.
This is the house you came home to.

Los Angeles, CA

☿

At an Evening Picnic with Will and Morgan in Echo Park. It Rained!

After Du Fu

I.

Sunset's the time to take the boat out,
when the drunks settle on their benches
and the lakeside vendors are closing up
their stalls of psychedelic fruit.

But while Morgan flips another beer cap
and Will flames another fluff of hash,
a drifting, lost-from-home, raincloud
darkens the sky. I must stop writing.

II.

And now it's raining, the benches soak,
fish surface to inch-long rain pelts
and children run in their flat wet clothes,
while mascaraed teens shed black tears.

Our rowboat scrapes against the lakeside,
a Corona bobs in the now-grey water,
and all the thirty yards to your front porch
the thunderstorm is autumn-in-June.

Los Angeles, CA

The Fish

Years after his death
my granddad announced his retirement
in a dream.

From here on
he would spend his days at the pub,
half his money

would go to us
and half his money to the *White Horse* till.
Why he told me this

after seven years
in the hardening ground, I don't know.
And why, in the dream,

after his long
declaration, he transformed into a fish
is hard to say.

A silver-skinned fish
I duly wrapped in baking parchment
and tied with a bow.

Or *cooking paper*,
as I scribbled – when I first awoke – on the back
of an envelope.

The Escapists

I come from a long line of escapists,
each of us born with the gift of shedding
handcuffs by shrinking the family wrists.
One Uncle watched the Titanic bedding

the soft Atlantic from the last lifeboat,
another woke this side of Little Bighorn
with just an insect-bite pimpling his throat,
a new coat, and his hair neatly shorn.

Then the family brides who vanish down
the O of their wedding bands year on year
and others, fathers, daughters: the clowns

who, as the time of reckoning drew near,
escaped the exam hall and the marriage vow
with the same excuse I give here now.

Marfa (I)

The air dry as if I just smoked a cigarette,
but no dust.

The desert curling round the buildings, the trees,
and feet that stray too far from the path.

Two cats divide up the different shade,
they do not like each other.

Both collect the evening's dead birds
that crash into the windows,

drawn by the cubes of polished steel to the glass
of the display hangar.

They eat like kings, but groom themselves like Caliban;
their matted hair snipped when they grow too feral.

I live quietly between people and feel the wind,
smoke and sit.

At night the light above the stoop rattles with insects,
but they are no more than a hum of wires.

My eyes adjust to the true dark above
and ahead in the flat desert

and in my staring the Milky Way, tall and inch-close,
does not prove me small

or lost, I greet it with my own slight ember
and exhale my smoke

as its smoke of stars relaxes casually.
The insects click at their impossible task

and I live within myself.

Marfa (II)

The swifts arrive in Marfa, they will be through a few days
and pass. They cover the power lines as if some spore has
come to germination. Small crescent inquisitions, they
examine me on the stoop. They want the ember in my
cigarette and the secret of the grey breath my mouth exhales.
They are gods of the little thunder, they might steal from me
and slip back into their crowd.

In the courtyard white rinds of bark curl from the birches.
The swifts fly among them looping, landing and revisiting
their flights. They are planning something. The trees idle
in the desert winds, their linen torn and falling. The birds
are teasing them for their stiffness, their Southern manners,
their old traditions. *Look: your time is done*, they say, *no
husbands now are coming home.*

Marfa, TX

Elm Hill

Long eye of dawn,
my spindle cigarette

matched by a spire's
half compass-needle,

the moisture
in the windows like settled snow.

I woke in the night
once at Portland Street

and snapped
pictures on an old Pentax –

I never developed –
of the paint-through-water

dawn,
orange like the fruit through glass.

Now, upward,
among the bird song,

the first or last car
cuts its engine –

lifted stylus –
then the birds' silence,

a shuffle of keys.
Taken through the night

by whatever carries us,
the black tree's

dry point,
dark cloud

and lighter white and rose behind,
our bodies

moisten in their beds
like bread.

I've listened too long
to the same feeling,

the birds with their
repetitions;

the thin-necked dove
on the roof top,

the aerials and weathervane;
how the colour thaws

green,
green-lemon

out of the black leaves;
the long straight jet trails

purposeful, caught by light,
strewn

as pale fleece;
the white paper of my cigarette

left outside on the step,
and the plume

of warm air from a furnace
at roof height.

Mercury

Sweet child the birds announce you as you pass,
the field is half sunlight and half shadow,
deep polarized green, bright glare on glass,

the sky flawless and blue as the ice floe.
Taking ten steps of the path as your own,
your feet make music with the grass below.

These months together are ours alone,
where I must play father-mother to your self
then deliver you to your mother's home.

Your legs kick out like a newborn calf,
you shriek and gulp the laughter of the air;
you braid the shadow and the sunlit half,

and when your absence is running there
you turn and flick the gold light of your hair.

White Birds

Each day my daughter comes up to the window
and points towards the birds. *Burr burr* she calls
    to gulls above or starlings below.

The picture is different this morning though,
the sky and lawns have lined themselves with snow.
She props on toes and watches the flakes fall

    onto clothesline and boundary wall.
She calls to them *burr burr* as they stall
and shoulder in the grey sky. She does not know.

Beacon, NY